A Woman's Workshop
—on—
PHILIPPIANS

Margaret and Paul Fromer

Lamplighter Books Grand Rapids, Michigan
Zondervan Publishing House

Lamplighter Books are published by Zondervan Publishing House, 1415 Lake Drive, S.E., Grand Rapids, Michigan 49506

A WOMAN'S WORKSHOP ON PHILIPPIANS
Copyright © 1982 by The Zondervan Corporation
Grand Rapids, Michigan

Library of Congress Cataloging in Publication Data
Fromer, Margaret.
   A woman's workshop on Philippians.

     1. Bible. N.T. Philippians—Study. 2. Women—Religious life. I. Fromer, Paul. II. Title.
BS2705.5.F76   227'.606   82-2662
ISBN 0-310-44771-2   AACR2

Edited by Jean Syswerda

Printed in the United States of America

85 86 87 88 — 10 9 8 7 6 5

CONTENTS

PAUL'S LETTER TO THE PHILIPPIANS

Why is Philippians so helpful to women facing problems related to their role in society, boredom, anxiety, and depression?

Perhaps it is because today women are searching out their roots. When they discern the crucial role women played at Philippi, they are especially at home in the letter written to the congregation there and are responsive to its teaching.

The church at Philippi (and the city itself) counted heavily on women and was concerned for them. One history book even notes that, in the Roman province where Philippi was located, women were known to have "built temples, founded cities, . . . commanded armies[!], held fortresses, and acted on occasion as regents or even co-rulers" (according to Tarn and Griffith).

How was the church at Philippi started? By women. A handful of them were meeting weekly to pray when God sent the apostle Paul to their city. One of them was a businesswoman who marketed purple fabric; she became the first person to trust herself to Christ there. And in whose house did the fledgling church begin to meet? In hers.

In his letter, Paul also names two other women who, he says, "contended at my side in the cause of the gospel." Their relation with him was so close he calls them "fellow workers."

Through the Philippian letter, women today can find help with at least five problems. One concerns their *role in life*. "Shall I stay at home and serve? Or shall I 'develop my potential' by pursuing a career?" Paul faced his own identity crisis in Philippians when he was boxed up in prison, facing possible death. He found purpose in the character of Christ, in relationships, and in God's control over his life.

Many women are *bored* with routine. "I'm awfully tired of staying at home talking with small kids," one said. Philippians discusses creative involvement with people. The very fact of studying with other women may stimulate outside-the-home relationships that restore inside-the-home enthusiasm.

Anxiety is a close, if unwanted, companion to many today. Women worry about drink, drugs, sex, and war. They are often frightened by the violence of our times and the possibility of hard times up ahead. To them Paul speaks of peace and puts hard times in perspective. In fact he was facing the threat of death by execution as he wrote.

A fearfully large number of today's women at some time face serious *depression*. It may dog their steps for months or even years. Paul was beset by sorrows too. Yet his letter to the Philippians is marked, as no other he wrote, by joy. Not that he clenched his teeth, forced a smile, and said fifty times rapidly, "I am happy." Rather he had to learn to be joyful. We'll find that this involved self-evaluation and relationships with others. But most of all Paul found joy in living union with Christ.

This suggests a last question women are asking today: *"Just who is Christ,* really? When can I count on him?" Is he simply some other-worldly mystic in white bedsheet and halo? Or is he a tough, gutsy, gentle servant? Fact is, Philippians is full of Christ, so we'll learn a great deal about who he really is.

As we do this, it's quite likely that some who use this study guide will find that a relationship with Christ is the most important treasure they can possess and the key to life as it was meant to be lived.

To be as accurate as possible on such important material, we have referred constantly, in our private study, though not formally in the guide, to the Greek text of Philippians, because Paul wrote in Greek. And we have tried to give fair attention to its theology. This letter, for instance, includes one of the most exalted overviews of the nature of Christ found in the New Testament (Philippians 2:1–11).

Also we have given heed to the insights of contemporary psychology, which has opened up interesting ways of looking at personality. When refined by biblical standards, we have found that these insights offer decided help to hurting people.

We have discovered that the writing of these Bible studies has been valuable to our marriage. Philippians has provided many joyful hours of discussion, argument, and insight.

As we studied, we felt uplifted partly because we wrote most of this guide at what must, at seven thousand feet above sea level, be one of the more heavenly of the national parks—Sequoia. Many of the college students serving the public there gave us their ideas on the passages under study. Of special help were Ruth Fromer and Mark Lee.

On occasion we found ourselves overwhelmed by the majesty of the Father and the helpfulness of Jesus Christ and the Holy Spirit. Perhaps it could be said that we experienced the middle-aged equivalent of a title couched in collegiate slang that Mark proposed: "Flip Out on Philippians."

GETTING THE MOST FROM GROUP STUDY

If we agree on a few ground rules, we will benefit more from the study:

1. **Stick to the passage.** The Philippians had only Paul's letter. As a master writer, he didn't assume a lot but explained what he meant as he wrote. So we don't have to rush around the New Testament finding verses that "shed light" on this book. Take it as a self-contained unit, and your study will be more profitable. Those who are new to Bible study won't feel overwhelmed by ignorance.

2. **Be thoughtful.** Suppose someone hesitantly offers an opinion you disagree with. The way you respond can make or break the study, so disagree agreeably. And if you remember that the court of final appeal for settling differences of opinion is the passage you are studying that week, all the members

can discuss an opinion on an equal footing. This gives the group a relaxed air in which discovery can flourish.

3. **If you can't come . . .** As the weeks proceed, members of a group begin to count on one another. If you will not be there, phone ahead to that week's hostess. This helps the group adjust to your absence. But hurry back!

4. **"How much should I say?"** A good group lets you operate at your own pace. But since some express themselves easily and some only with difficulty, it helps to strike a balance. If you talk easily, exercise restraint or you'll dominate the study. If you are reserved, risk being a little forward. Surprisingly, God may have as much to say to the group through the quiet people as through the talkative ones. Also, since expression makes *im*pression, it's wise to establish a spirit in the group in which hesitant people feel free to speak.

5. **"We didn't get to apply the passage."** A little planning will avoid the problem of neglecting application. The studies are put together to seek out the passage's main point and then apply it. Only with this last step does God reach the goal he has in the passage. We read that Scripture is to be "profitable" (2 Timothy 3:16). This is so only when we go beyond intellectual information to personal response. As the members talk over how to apply the passage, they help one another. Pace yourself so that you get to the last questions in each study. They are designed to help you make the passage personal.

6. **Be a hostess.** You'll feel more a part of the group, and so get more from the discussion, if you ask the group to meet occasionally in your own home. But keep arrangements simple.

7. **"Lead? Me?"** Almost anyone can lead this kind of a study. You will need to prepare carefully, but the questions in the study guide really are answered in the passage, so the group will not be hard to lead. Read on for a few clues.

THE PLEASURE OF LEADING A STUDY

Most groups pass the leadership around to several people. If you have never led before, watch what the leaders are doing. Soon you will probably find that the time is ripe for you to lead too. Here are some clues to doing a good job.

1. **Start early.** Try to start preparing about two weeks before you lead, so you can get familiar with the passage and questions. Crash programs produce jittery leaders. But if you give yourself time, God will make you at home in the study. And as you apply the material to yourself and live with it for a while, you will have a better sense of the force of the passage.

2. **Study the passage first.** Don't read the study questions first, but rather study the passage directly. Each paragraph usually has a main point—see if you can find it. Look for important contrasts or parallels. If there is an effect, look for its

cause. If there is controversy, spot the two sides. If there is a problem, state it in a sentence and then look for the passage's solution. If Paul illustrates a point by referring to a person or situation, try to grasp the illustration. See what you learn about God and about his relation to us. Are you moved to prayer? Then pray.

3. **Answer the guide's questions.** Now it is time to use the prepared questions. Write out your answers in the blanks; if your answer comes from one verse, note its number. Put the applications you discover immediately into practice.

4. **Consider these discussion tips.** During the week before the study, read over the section, "Getting the Most From Group Study" and "The Pleasure of Leading a Study." Since it's important to *lead* a discussion, *not teach* a lesson, ask questions and let the passage supply the answers. If the group needs help, rephrase a question if necessary, but don't answer it. If the group sees that you believe the answers are in the passage, they will take heart and look there. Otherwise they may try to read an answer on your face or wait for you to provide it. What a member sees for herself is often what she finds most profitable, so give her a chance.

5. **Start the study on time.** God has great things in store for the group, so begin with confidence in him. He has much more at stake in the study than you do. Ask someone to open in prayer, make any use you want of the guide's introductory paragraph (or ignore it), ask someone to read the passage, and pose your first question.

6. **Plan on an hour for the study.** Keep track of time as you ask questions. The later questions are for application, so try to reserve about a third of your time for them. To find them valu-

able, though, the group must first find the specifics of the passage and the principles they add up to, based on the earlier questions.

7. **Don't fear silence.** After all, someone may be thinking! Of course, blank silences are useless, but "working" silences are crucial. If the members are studying the passage to find answers, don't rush them. They may also need a little time to find courage to speak.

8. **Complete the whole study each time.** If time is getting short, cut out a couple of questions of lesser importance. If the discussion is turning into a bull session or is too absorbed in one point, gently but firmly point out that time is passing and there are still verses to study and questions to answer. If someone wants to spend more time on a certain point, offer to get together with her later. She might also like to consult a short commentary on the troublesome point. We recommend *The New Bible Commentary*, F. Davidson, ed. (Eerdmans) and *The New Bible Dictionary*, J. D. Douglas, ed. (Eerdmans).

9. **Answers at the back of the book?** It was with fear and trembling that we included answers in the "Notes to Leaders." If you look at them before you study the passage and answer the questions all by yourself, they could destroy your discussion. We decided to include them so that if you did not see how much there was in each passage but were stopping too soon, you could take a second look. But don't, don't, don't try to teach those answers to the group. They are provided only for your private reference when you prepare.

Incidentally, where there are troublesome spots you will encounter in leading the passage, we have included hints at the appropriate spot in the leader's notes. They offer ways to handle tough leadership problems.

10. **Your group will learn to work together.** A kind of division of labor will occur in the course of time. You can encourage the group along these lines:

a. On occasion ask for more than one response to a question. Ask, "Does anyone else see something here?" or "Mary, do you agree?"

b. Appreciate each person's answer. Her answer may or may not be "right," but show her you are for her as she tries to answer.

c. Don't restate all the answers in your own words, as if you, not Scripture, were the authority. If you think the response is not complete or clear, however, ask whoever answered to state it in other words. You might do this for her if she can't, or you could ask the group to clarify the answer.

d. Ask questions that will help members explain one another's answers. Ideally members should evaluate, defend, and develop one another's ideas. This is a *real discussion,* not one where the questions are disguised devices by which the leader runs the meeting like a top sergeant. When you ask a more complex question, encourage reaction to the answer and reaction to the reaction, if there is time and if the discussion continues to be profitable.

11. **Don't forget God.** We are too sinful and narrow to understand God. But he delights to reveal the meaning of his Scripture—it's why he gives it to us. So have confidence in him; he wants to help you study in advance and then lead. When it's all over, thank him for what he did.

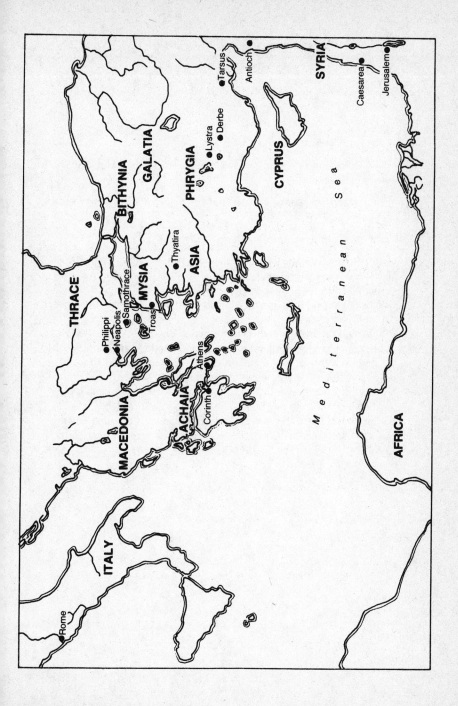

¹Paul and Timothy, servants of Christ Jesus,

To all the saints in Christ Jesus at Philippi, together with the overseers and deacons:

²Grace and peace to you from God our Father and the Lord Jesus Christ.

Thanksgiving and Prayer

³I thank my God every time I remember you. ⁴In all my prayers for all of you, I always pray with joy ⁵because of your partnership in the gospel from the first day until now, ⁶being confident of this, that he who began a good work in you will carry it on to completion until the day of Christ Jesus.

⁷It is right for me to feel this way about all of you, since I have you in my heart; for whether I am in chains or defending and confirming the gospel, all of you share in God's grace with me. ⁸God can testify how I long for all of you with the affection of Christ Jesus.

⁹And this is my prayer: that your love may abound more and more in knowledge and depth of insight, ¹⁰so that you may be able to discern what is best and may be pure and blameless until the day of Christ, ¹¹filled with the fruit of righteousness that comes through Jesus Christ—to the glory and praise of God.

—*Philippians 1:1–11*

Quiet time questions (Philippians 1:1–11)

1. What does Paul find to rejoice in about the Philippians?

2. How can it be said that the Philippians, hundreds of miles from Paul, are his partners in the gospel and in God's grace?

3. Suppose you heard that someone you respected was enthusiastic about God's work in you. What effect would this have on your growth in Christ?

4. In practical terms, how can you show other Christians that you are a partner with them in God's grace?

STUDY ONE

Acts 16:6–40: Philippians 1:1–11

Sometimes the demands of the Christian life seem like an endless row of brownstone houses—dull, motionless, staring.

The fizz seems absent from our Coke and only the pallid taste of guilt remains.

It's a shock to read A. W. Tozer's comment, "God is easy to live with."

"No," we say. "That's not right; he's hard to live with. I'm so weary of trying to measure up, I don't know where to turn."

After a quick look at the record of Paul's visit to the city of Philippi, we may begin to find some clues on where to turn. And as we go on to the opening verses of his letter to the believers there, we may even wonder if he didn't have an eye cocked on us too.

Read Acts 16:6–24 aloud and locate on the map the places mentioned in the text.

1. For what reasons did Paul go to Philippi? _____

_____

_____

2. What clues do you find to the length of time Paul stayed in Philippi? _____

_____

_____

3. a. Contrast the welcome given by Lydia and the prayer group with that given by the owners of the slave girl. (Who were they? What were they doing? How did they react?) _____

_____

_____

_____

   b. What reasons are given for the response of each?

_____

_____

Read Acts 16:25–40 aloud.
4. How did God now back up Paul as he obeyed the vision of verses 9–10? _____

_____

_____

5. a. What effect might Paul's experiences have had on the new church's attitude toward adversity? _____

_____

_____

b. What effect might these experiences have had on their attitude toward Paul? _____

_____

_____

Read Philippians 1:1–11 aloud.
6. What clues do you find in the salutation (vv. 1–2) about what has happened to the Christian group at Philippi during Paul's absence? _____

_____

_____

_____

7. What phrases indicate the strength of Paul's affection for the Philippians? _____

_____

_____

_____

8. For what reasons does Paul say it is appropriate for him to feel so enthusiastic about the Philippians? _____

_____

_____

Focus on verses 9–11.
9. How do these verses define the ways in which God will complete the good work he has begun in them? _____

_____

_____

_____

10. How does Paul's life illustrate the qualities he wanted to see develop in the Philippians? (Use Acts 16 and Philippians 1:1–8.) _____

_____

_____

_____

_____

11. As you look at yourself or others in this group, how do you see God bringing his good work to completion?

_____

_____

_____

Follow-up project:

Write out in your own words (a paraphrase) Paul's prayer for the Philippians (1:9–11). Now choose a Christian you know and pray this prayer for that person.

Paul's Chains Advance the Gospel

¹²Now I want you to know, brothers, that what has happened to me has really served to advance the gospel. ¹³As a result, it has become clear throughout the whole palace guard and to everyone else that I am in chains for Christ. ¹⁴Because of my chains, most of the brothers in the Lord have been encouraged to speak the word of God more courageously and fearlessly.

¹⁵It is true that some preach Christ out of envy and rivalry, but others out of good will. ¹⁶The latter do so in love, knowing that I am put here for the defense of the gospel. ¹⁷The former preach Christ out of selfish ambition, not sincerely, supposing that they can stir up trouble for me while I am in chains. ¹⁸But what does it matter? The important thing is that in every way, whether from false motives or true, Christ is preached. And because of this I rejoice.

Yes, and I will continue to rejoice, ¹⁹for I know that through your prayers and the help given by the Spirit of Jesus Christ, what has happened to me will turn out for my deliverance. ²⁰I eagerly expect and hope that I will in no way be ashamed, but will have sufficient courage so that now as always Christ will be exalted in my body, whether by life or by death. ²¹For to me, to live is Christ and to die is gain. ²²If I am to go on living in the body, this will mean fruitful labor for me. Yet what shall I choose? I do not know! ²³I am torn between the two: I desire to depart and be with Christ, which is better by far; ²⁴but it is more necessary for you that I remain in the body. ²⁵Convinced of this, I know that I will remain, and I will continue with all of you for your progress and joy in the faith, ²⁶so that through my being with you again your joy in Christ Jesus will overflow on account of me.

—Philippians 1:12–26

Quiet time questions (Philippians 1:12–26)

1. Think of some words or phrases that describe Paul's mood as he writes.

2. In verses 1–11 we noticed the warmth of feeling between Paul and the Philippians. What clues to their relationship do you see in 1:12–26?

3. A person with a lot of drive, when confined to prison, might get to the place where she sits in the corner, pulls a blanket over her head, and waits for the end. How does Paul show wisdom in maintaining good mental health while he is in prison (habits of thought and action)?

4. What habits can you develop now that would stand you in good stead in time of conflict?

A verse worth memorizing: Philippians 1:21

For to me, to live is Christ and to die is gain.

STUDY TWO

Philippians 1:12–26

Think of the last time you cut your finger and drew blood. How long did healing take? That question, doctors say, provides a good test of your health.

We all cut ourselves. We all get sick. But if the cut runs raw for weeks or the sickness lingers on and on, we learn something about the state of our health.

The same test applies to our mental health. Life constantly confronts us with shocks. The postman brings an unexpected bill. The principal phones us to come for our son. The doctor visibly screws up his courage before telling us the results of the lab test. Mental health is not the absence of responses like fright or despair, but rather it concerns recovery. What kind of resources can we draw on to bounce back when the roof falls in?

It fell in for Paul at Rome. He was a hard-driving person with a lot of fizz and flourish. Then someone put him in a box (a jail), chopped him off from normal life, and threatened him with death. How long would it take you to adjust to such a shock? In today's passage, we get some help from observing how Paul responded.

1. Before reading Philippians 1:12–26, consider this question: Suppose someone you loved, while traveling in a distant country, was arrested and held for trial. Being cut off from information about him, what worries would you have for him? _____

_____

_____

_____

Read Philippians 1:12–26 aloud.
2. As you look through these verses, what do you see that could have caused Paul to be despondent? _____

_____

_____

_____

3. What, according to the passage, are the positive results of Paul's imprisonment? _____

_____

_____

_____

4. Why did Paul's imprisonment make the Christians in Rome more bold instead of more fearful? _____

_____

_____

5. What evidences do you see in verses 12–18 of the power of the gospel? _____

_____

_____

_____

6. a. What attitudes in yourself or what outward circumstances make it less than ideal for you to talk about Christ? _____

_____

_____

b. How might verses 12–18 encourage you to talk about Christ in circumstances that are not ideal? _____

_____

_____

_____

Read Philippians 1:19–26 aloud.

7. Paul has been rejoicing in the midst of his present circumstances. As he looks toward his uncertain future, what further opportunities does he see for rejoicing? (Use all of verses 19–26 for your answer.) _____

_____

_____

_____

_____

_____

8. a. According to this passage, what are the overriding purposes of Paul's life? _____

_____

_____

b. How does the relationship to Christ suggested by these goals help Paul rejoice in the face of uncertain and fearful circumstances? _____

_____

_____

_____

9. In the mixture of our attitudes toward death, various fears play an important part. What fears or sorrows are you aware of in yourself? _____

_____

_____

_____

10. Consider the principles by which Paul lived. How can we begin to rejoice, even as we acknowledge our fears and sorrows? _____

_____

_____

_____

11. Living as well as dying has its fears. One of these is the fear of a routine that leaves us bored and deprives us of self-respect. How have you found that a relation with Jesus helps you beat the boredom of routine? _____

_____

_____

_____

_____

Follow-up project:
   1. Everyone lives in various "worlds." A woman might, for instance, have these worlds: her family, her neighborhood, her occupation, her church, and her friendships. Jot down several things in each of these areas that are causes for rejoicing.

   2. Paul was able to rejoice even when he was under extreme pressure. Think of one area in which things don't seem to be working out for you as you'd like. Prayerfully list ways that this pressure point can lead to opportunities for rejoicing.

   3. Using your two lists, spend time thanking and praising God.

[27]Whatever happens, conduct yourselves in a manner worthy of the gospel of Christ. Then, whether I come and see you or only hear about you in my absence, I will know that you stand firm in one spirit, contending as one man for the faith of the gospel [28]without being frightened in any way by those who oppose you. This is a sign to them that they will be destroyed, but that you will be saved—and that by God. [29]For it has been granted to you on behalf of Christ not only to believe on him, but also to suffer for him, [30]since you are going through the same struggle you saw I had, and now hear that I still have.

Imitating Christ's Humility

[1]If you have any encouragement from being united with Christ, if any comfort from his love, if any fellowship with the Spirit, if any tenderness and compassion, [2]then make my joy complete by being like-minded, having the same love, being one in spirit and purpose. [3]Do nothing out of selfish ambition or vain conceit, but in humility consider others better than yourselves. [4]Each of you should look not only to your own interests, but also to the interests of others.

[5]Your attitude should be the same as that of Christ Jesus:

[6]Who, being in very nature God,
did not consider equality with God something to be grasped,
[7]but made himself nothing,
taking the very nature of a servant,
being made in human likeness.
[8]And being found in appearance as a man,
he humbled himself
and became obedient to death—
even death on a cross!
[9]Therefore God exalted him to the highest place
and gave him the name that is above every name,
[10]that at the name of Jesus every knee should bow,
in heaven and on earth and under the earth,
[11]and every tongue confess that Jesus Christ is Lord,
to the glory of God the Father.

—Philippians 1:27–2:11

Quiet time questions (Philippians 1:27–2:1)

1. Why might the Philippians be tempted to conduct themselves in a manner unworthy of the gospel?

2. What incentives does Paul identify to stimulate them to live a life worthy of the gospel?

3. Philippians 2:1–11 is one of the New Testament's four most important statements on Christ's character. (John 1, Colossians 1, and Hebrews 1 are the other three.) What practical problem at Philippi is Paul trying to solve by this exalted description?

4. Think about what Christ did until God gives you a sense of what it cost. Praise him.

Verses worth memorizing: Philippians 2:3–5

The central passage in the book is 2:1–11 and well worth memorizing if you want to carry the Book of Philippians with you after we have finished the study.

STUDY THREE

Philippians 1:27–2:11

"Humility—I hate it!"

About ten of us in a Great Books discussion group happened to be studying Christ's Sermon on the Mount (Matthew 5–7) that Thursday night. Very early it had become clear that Christ was arguing for humility.

"'Poor in spirit,' 'turn the other cheek.' Jesus just wants us to be milquetoasts," one person exclaimed. "What's so noble about being everybody's doormat?"

A women with executive ability (mother of six) seconded his motion. "Why sit around wringing our hands?" she asked. "I admire people with 'git up and git'!"

We read Christ's call to "love" or "unselfishness" and nod our heads in agreement. But when he calls for humility, don't we feel the hackles rise?

Strange, then, that Paul, in one of the New Testament's foremost statements on who Christ is, makes a big point of his humility. Could it be that humility means something different

34

in the Bible from what it has come to mean to us today?

Read Philippians 1:27–2:4 aloud.
1. What terms in Philippians 1:27–30 suggest that the Philippians were under fire from strong opponents?

_____

_____

2. How would you describe the spirit Paul wishes to see them exhibit as they face their enemies? _____

_____

3. a. In Philippians 2:1–4, what attitudes does Paul say interfere with achieving necessary unity? _____

_____

_____

b. Why do you think this selfish life contradicts a true commitment to Christ? _____

_____

_____

_____

4. a. How do the influences of verse 1 lead us toward unity rather than selfishness? _____

_____

_____

b. How does the humility of verses 3–4 lead to unity?

_____

_____

_____

Read Philippians 2:5–11 aloud.

5. Before we study the passage in detail, suggest some ways it appears from these verses that Christ provides an ideal example of the humility Paul has in mind for the Philippians. _____

_____

_____

6. a. In verses 6–8 what phrases describe the high position Christ formerly held? _____

_____

b. What phrases describe the low position he voluntarily took? _____

_____

_____

7. a. What rights and satisfactions do you suppose Christ set aside to become a man? _____

_____

_____

b. When Christ added human nature to his divine nature and became a servant, what limitations do you suppose he accepted? _____

_____

_____

_____

8. In what ways do you think the exaltation of Christ (vv. 9–11) would influence the Philippians to stand unitedly and resist their opponents? _____

_____

_____

_____

_____

9. In what ways did Christ's display of humility go beyond his merely honest assessment of his own worth? _____

_____

_____

10. What in this passage shows that the biblical call for humility does not mean we are to become "doormats" for others? _____

_____

_____

_____

11. a. What are the areas in which your own ambition or your sense of competence tends to stray across the line into selfish ambition or conceit? _____

_____

_____

b. How do the teachings of this passage help you to restrain yourself in these cases? _____

_____

_____

12. Suppose that the youth program in your church had been spiritually weak for many years. Suppose also that after praying about it you have come to the conviction that the only answer is for the church to hire a part-time youth director who has a spiritual ministry to young people. You propose this to the church and encounter great

opposition from those who think youth work should be done without pay by laymen in the church. What guidelines can you find in Philippians 2:1–11 that would help you to check yourself to see if in your enthusiasm you are making the mistakes that Paul cautions against?

_____

_____

_____

_____

Follow-up project:

One way to "look to the interests of others" is to consider their needs and discover how to meet them. Another way to pay attention to others is to look at the notable traits of character that commend them. For example, a homemaker may arrange her time poorly but be exceptionally kind with children—her own and others.

1. This week think of three people you find hard to get along with and list as many positive qualities of each as you can.

2. Pray, thanking the Lord for these gifts he has given to them.

3. Think of one way to express your appreciation to each of these three people.

Shining as Stars

[12]Therefore, my dear friends, as you have always obeyed—not only in my presence, but now much more in my absence—continue to work out your salvation with fear and trembling, [13]for it is God who works in you to will and to act according to his good purpose.

[14]Do everything without complaining or arguing, [15]so that you may become blameless and pure, children of God without fault in a crooked and depraved generation, in which you shine like stars in the universe [16]as you hold out the word of life—in order that I may boast on the day of Christ that I did not run or labor for nothing. [17]But even if I am being poured out like a drink offering on the sacrifice and service coming from your faith, I am glad and rejoice with all of you. [18]So you too should be glad and rejoice with me.

Timothy and Epaphroditus

[19]I hope in the Lord Jesus to send Timothy to you soon, that I also may be cheered when I receive news about you. [20]I have no one else like him, who takes a genuine interest in your welfare. [21]For everyone looks out for his own interests, not those of Jesus Christ. [22]But you know that Timothy has proved himself, because as a son with his father he has served with me in the work of the gospel. [23]I hope, therefore, to send him as soon as I see how things go with me. [24]And I am confident in the Lord that I myself will come soon.

[25]But I think it is necessary to send back to you Epaphroditus, my brother, fellow worker and fellow soldier, who is also your messenger, whom you sent to take care of my needs. [26]For he longs for all of you and is distressed because you heard he was ill. [27]Indeed he was ill, and almost died. But God had mercy on him, and not on him only but also on me, to spare me sorrow upon sorrow. [28]Therefore I am all the more eager to send him, so that when you see him again you may be glad and I may have less anxiety. [29]Welcome him in the Lord with great joy, and honor men like him, [30]because he almost died for the work of Christ, risking his life to make up for the help you could not give me.

—*Philippians 2:12–30*

Quiet time questions (Philippians 2:12–30)

1. Read 2:12–18. Paul says in verse 13 that God is at work in us. What is the relation between this and the following two things: the complaining mentioned in verse 14 and the rejoicing in verses 17–18?

2. It has been said that Christian fellowship is less a "gooey feeling" than a combination of hard work, cold cash, and companionship. How do you see this illustrated by Timothy and Epaphroditus in verses 19–30?

3. a. Make a list of some of the things Paul wants the Philippians to do in verses 12–30.

   b. Put a check beside those that you find pose a special problem.

   c. For the items checked, what help do you think you need from God in the matter of will as well as of action (v. 13)?

   d. Ask him for this help.

STUDY FOUR

Philippians 2:12–30

On a sunny spring day, the part-time pastor of a small church was mopping out the entrance hall. A well-dressed woman walked up the steps and said, "I see by your sign that you invite people to come and have fellowship with you."

"That's right," the pastor said. "We have a lot of Christian fellowship here."

"My husband and I have been looking for a place like that. We think it's so important for people to have warm fellowship."

"You're right," the pastor said, placing the mop handle in her hand. "Let's start right now."

Fellowship. What does it include? A warm feeling? Doctrinal agreement? The apostle Paul wouldn't disagree, but he seems to take it a step further. He puts mop handles in our hands too.

Read Philippians 2:12–13 aloud.

1. To discover the basic command Paul now calls on the Philippians to obey, reread verses 1–11, which we studied last time. What is his central instruction in those verses? _____

_____

_____

2. Picture a Philippian who says, "It was hard enough to obey God when Paul was here; it's much harder now that he's gone." How does Paul deal with such a person?

_____

_____

_____

3. What is the cause of the "fear and trembling" at this relationship with God? _____

_____

_____

_____

4. a. Mention a characteristic of God that inspires awe in you. _____

_____

b. How might this awe toward God support your obedience to him? _____

_____

_____

_____

Read Philippians 2:14–30 aloud.

5. What examples of sacrificial service does Paul commend? _____

_____

_____

Focus on verses 14–18.

6. How does the distinction between the church and the world become blurred if the church is characterized by selfish complaining? _____

_____

_____

_____

7. What reasons does Paul find to rejoice in the face of his possible death?

Note to reader: Paul saw the obedience of the Philippians to be like an offering to God that arose from their faith. In particular they put their faith on the line by sacrificially sending Epaphroditus with a gift (2:25–30; 4:14–17). It was a risk to declare their partnership openly because Paul might be judged a criminal who deserved execution. The friends of such a person would be suspect.

What is the meaning of a drink offering? In the Old Testament, when a person offered a costly sacrifice to God, he might also pour out on the ground nearby a drink offering that was in addition to the main offering (Numbers 15:1–10). In our passage, Paul views his possible death as a drink offering to go along with the "sacrifice" presented by the Philippians.

_____

_____

_____

_____

8. Consider the ways you complain and argue with God as you serve others. In light of the passage, how do you think you can turn your complaining into rejoicing?

_____

_____

_____

Focus on verses 19–24.

9. How does Timothy's character serve to illustrate the attitudes Paul has been urging on the Philippians in this chapter? _____

_____

_____

_____

Read Philippians 2:25–30 aloud again.

10. In order to carry out his mission effectively, what attitudes would Epaphroditus have needed? (Support your answers from the text, vv. 25–30.) _____

_____

_____

_____

11. The warm feeling we have for other Christians is part of fellowship. (See 1:7 and 2:12.) What more should true fellowship include? Base your answers on the example of Epaphroditus. _____

_____

_____

_____

12. How do you go about getting the willingness to be one with other people rather than to be merely independent? (Use all of chapter 2 for your answer.) _____

_____

_____

_____

_____

_____

Follow-up project:

Paul has been showing, by illustration as well as instruction, that fellowship goes beyond feeling into action. Your Bible study group is a small fellowship of people who have a chance to express their feelings of concern for one another through action. They can help each other during a crisis (illness), or with special projects (painting the bedroom or cleaning the windows), or in routine jobs (weekly housework or errands). Here is a two-step project for this week. It involves planning with one or two others and then doing what you plan:

Step 1: Split up into subgroups of two or three. Ask each person in your subgroup to share a matter in which she could use some service from the others. Each person in this small group should then choose one project to do for one of the others, or all may work together on one larger task.

Step 2: Do it.

No Confidence in the Flesh

¹Finally, my brothers, rejoice in the Lord! It is no trouble for me to write the same things to you again, and it is a safeguard for you.

²Watch out for those dogs, those men who do evil, those mutilators of the flesh. ³For it is we who are the circumcision, we who worship by the Spirit of God, who glory in Christ Jesus, and who put no confidence in the flesh— ⁴though I myself have reasons for such confidence.

If anyone else thinks he has reasons to put confidence in the flesh, I have more: ⁵circumcised on the eighth day, of the people of Israel, of the tribe of Benjamin, a Hebrew of Hebrews; in regard to the law, a Pharisee; ⁶as for zeal, persecuting the church; as for legalistic righteousness, faultless.

⁷But whatever was to my profit I now consider loss for the sake of Christ. ⁸What is more, I consider everything a loss compared to the surpassing greatness of knowing Christ Jesus my Lord, for whose sake I have lost all things. I consider them rubbish, that I may gain Christ ⁹and be found in him, not having a righteousness of my own that comes from the law, but that which is through faith in Christ—the righteousness that comes from God and is by faith. ¹⁰I want to know Christ and the power of his resurrection and the fellowship of sharing in his sufferings, becoming like him in his death, ¹¹and so, somehow, to atttain to the resurrection from the dead.

—*Philippians 3:1–11*

Quiet time questions (Philippians 3:1–11)

1. Verse 1 calls us to rejoice. What does the passage identify that we can rejoice in?

2. What are we saying about Christ when we trust him instead of ourselves?

3. In verses 5–6 Paul lists a number of things that got in the way of his trusting Christ. Identify some things that tempt you to do the same today.

4. Verses 10–11 describe ways in which Paul is growing in the Lord. In what ways are you coming to experience Christ more in these areas?

A verse worth memorizing: Philippians 3:8 (or 3:8–9)

What is more, I consider everything a loss compared to the surpassing greatness of knowing Jesus Christ my Lord, for whose sake I have lost all things. I consider them rubbish, that I might gain Christ (v. 8).

and be found in him, not having a righteousness of my own that comes from the law, but that which is through faith in Christ—the righteousness that comes from God and is by faith (v. 9).

STUDY FIVE

Philippians 3:1–11

Many people say America is too "secular." Could be.

But as we talk with neighbors and business acquaintances, we probably find that almost everyone has at least a mild interest in God. A recent Gallup Poll bears this out, showing that 94 percent believe in some kind of god.

The apostle Paul never had the problem of being too secular. Nor had he been only vaguely religious. Far from it. Rather, he had been wildly religious—too religious, in fact, to be a Christian. His religion had been like a lump of undigested beef that caused him acute indigestion.

That may seem odd to us, but our religiousness too may be keeping us from Christ. In this week's passage, Paul explains from bitter personal experience.

Read Philippians 3:1–3 aloud.
1. Considering Paul's words in verse 2, what impressions do you form of the men Paul criticizes? _____

_____

_____

2. What contrast do you see between those who trust in the physical act of circumcision (v. 2) and those Paul describes in verse 3? _____

_____

_____

_____

3. According to verse 3, how would Paul answer a Jew who told the Philippians, "You must go through the ritual of circumcision to be acceptable to God"? (After answering this question, glance at Romans 2:28–29.) _____

_____

_____

_____

_____

Focus on verses 4–6.

> *Note:* Paul has just made a play on the word *circumcision.* He has suggested that the true circumcision are people who glory in Christ. The false circumcision are merely mutilators of the flesh. Now he makes a play on the word *flesh.* The flesh involved in physical circumcision becomes a symbol for all the wrong things in which we put our confidence.

Read Philippians 3:4–6 aloud.

4. Which of Paul's reasons for confidence refer to his religious pedigree and which to his religious performance?

_____

_____

5. With an eye on Paul's comments in verses 5–6,
   a. Mention ways people today rely on religious pedigree for standing with God. _____

   _____

   _____

   b. In what ways do we rely on our religious performance? _____

   _____

   _____

Read Philippians 3:7–11 aloud.
6. a. How did Paul come to treat these reasons for confidence? _____

   _____

   _____

   b. According to verses 8–9, why is confidence in pedigree and performance dangerous? _____

   _____

   _____

7. In what ways does the righteousness God gives us through faith in Christ differ from the righteousness of an upright life? _____

   _____

   _____

   _____

8. Paul counts not only his religious achievements as loss,

but *all* his reasons for self-confidence ("everything," v. 8). What are the things instead of Christ on which you are tempted to base your sense of worth or well-being?

_____

_____

_____

9. From your own experience, what did you do to make the shift from basing your life on your own righteousness to basing your life on the righteousness that is a gift from God? _____

_____

_____

_____

10. If you count all the other things as loss, what now do you have to live for? (Your answers should grow out of verses 10–11.) _____

_____

_____

_____

Follow-up project:
Think of a non-Christian friend who has a low self-image.

Using this passage as a source, write down some things you could tell your friend that could help him/her get over this inferiority.

Pressing on Toward the Goal

¹²Not that I have already obtained all this, or have already been made perfect, but I pressed on to take hold of that for which Christ Jesus took hold of me. ¹³Brothers, I do not consider myself yet to have taken hold of it. But one thing I do: Forgetting what is behind and straining toward what is ahead, ¹⁴I press on toward the goal to win the prize for which God has called me heavenward in Christ Jesus.

¹⁵All of us who are mature should take such a view of things. And if on some point you think differently, that too God will make clear to you. ¹⁶Only let us live up to what we have already attained.

¹⁷Join with others in following my example, brothers, and take note of those who live according to the pattern we gave you. ¹⁸For, as I have often told you before and now say again even with tears, many live as enemies of the cross of Christ. ¹⁹Their destiny is destruction, their god is their stomach, and their glory is in their shame. Their mind is on earthly things. ²⁰But our citizenship is in heaven. And we eagerly await a Savior from there, the Lord Jesus Christ, ²¹who, by the power that enables him to bring everything under his control, will transform our lowly bodies so that they will be like his glorious body.

¹Therefore, my brothers, you whom I love and long for, my joy and crown, that is how you should stand firm in the Lord, dear friends!

—*Philippians 3:12–4:1*

Quiet time questions (Philippians 3:12–4:1)

1. What does Paul admit not having yet perfected? (Use verses 10–11 for your answer.)

2. Phrases like "straining" and "I press on toward the goal" suggest the track and field events so popular in ancient Greece. In light of what Paul says, compare the faithful runner and the faithful Christian.

3. What has held you back from making an all-out effort?

4. What has it been like when God has freed you to make such an effort?

STUDY SIX

Philippians 3:12–4:1

"My Christian life? It's like warm Coca Cola—no fizz, flat." We all recall vital experiences with God that led to enthusiastic obedience. But now that may be only a memory. Yet God knows we face these slowing-down periods and offers help.

Paul has just said in verses 7–9 that all release is rooted in coming to the end of ourselves. Surprisingly, we may have to relearn this repeatedly in our Christian lives. Paul admits that he was once too religious to be a Christian. His achievements, even his religious ones, were actually obstacles to his relation to God, because they took the place of trusting Christ to make him right with God.

God brought him to see this, so Paul deliberately rejected every self-confidence and took his stand on the goodness of someone else: Christ. He stopped trying to nickel-and-dime his way into God's good graces; rather, swallowing his pride, he accepted a million-dollar gift from Christ—salvation that rested solely on Christ's achievements, not Paul's.

This was the real beginning of Paul's life. Captivated by Christ, he found himself wanting to do anything to please Christ and get to know him better. He identified with Christ. Christ became the root of Paul's enthusiasm.

In our passage this week, Paul starts by examining the all-out life he now leads by God's grace. A comparison occurs to him—the enthusiastic commitment of a runner in a race. No doubt the Philippians shared the common Greek love of track and field events just as we love sports today. Trusting Christ's righteousness and striving to know him are ways the Christian resembles the dedicated Olympic runner who has decided to "go for the gold."

Read Philippians 3:12–16 aloud.

> *Note:* The "this" Paul seeks to obtain refers back to verses 10–11. There he has said he wants to become more like Christ.

1. a. What are some of the feeling words you would use to describe the emotional tone of verses 12–16? _____

   _____

   b. What words or phrases give you this impression?

   _____

2. a. What does Paul deny and what does he affirm in verse 12? _____

   _____

   b. How do these compare with what he denies and affirms in verses 13–14? _____

   _____

   _____

   _____

3. In verses 12–16, what are the temptations Paul resists as he seeks to become more like Christ? _____

_____

_____

_____

4. One temptation Paul resists is to dwell on past mistakes. How do haunting past mistakes prevent you from pressing on? _____

_____

_____

_____

5. As Paul stands in the present looking over his shoulder at the past and ahead toward the future, what things make him optimistic? _____

_____

_____

6. Look at Philippians 1:6 and 2:13. What actions of God in your own life come to mind? How has he helped you to press on? _____

_____

_____

_____

Read Philippians 3:17–4:1 aloud.
7. What situation made Paul think a strong Christian model was necessary for the Philippians? _____

_____

_____

8. What satisfactions might these enemies of Christ say they were gaining by their way of life? (It might help to think of the enticements of some of today's TV ads.) _____

_____

_____

9. How does Paul contrast the two lifestyles? For each consider (a) the long term value, and (b) the consequences.

_____

_____

10. a. Describe a person whom God has used as a model in your Christian life. _____

_____

_____

b. What Bible passages has God especially used to instruct you? _____

_____

_____

c. What do you see as the relation between living models and written guidelines? _____

_____

11. Is this statement true? "It's not a question of *whether* we'll be a model to others, but rather it is a question of *what kind* of model we will be." Explain your answer.

_____

_____

_____

12. Think of a situation in which you have personally experi-

enced warm support from a more mature Christian, the sort Paul displays for the Philippians in 4:1. What effect has this had on you? _____

_____

_____

Follow-up project:
Most of us have such a low view of ourselves that we can't believe others would model themselves after us in any way, so we miss the joy and encouragement of knowing God has used us as models to others. Let's do two things to try to correct this:

1. Let's deliberately thank someone whose example God has used in our lives. This may be the person you thought of in answering question 10 or it may be someone else. We might say or write something like this: "You probably don't realize it, but when you said you were praying for your son, I realized I'd been worrying but not praying for *my* son. I want you to know God is using you in my life. Thank you."

2. Doing the first part of this project may help us to realize that God has used us, too, in someone else's life. We may have had either a great or a small influence. Think of someone you have helped and thank God for using you this way.

¹Therefore, my brothers, you whom I love and long for, my joy and crown, that is how you should stand firm in the Lord, dear friends!

Exhortations

²I plead with Euodia and I plead with Syntyche to agree with each other in the Lord. ³Yes, and I ask you, loyal yokefellow, help these women who have contended at my side in the cause of the gospel, along with Clement and the rest of my fellow workers, whose names are in the book of life.

⁴Rejoice in the Lord always. I will say it again: Rejoice! ⁵Let your gentleness be evident to all. The Lord is near. ⁶Do not be anxious about anything, but in everything, by prayer and petition, with thanksgiving, present your requests to God. ⁷And the peace of God, which transcends all understanding, will guard your hearts and your minds in Christ Jesus.

⁸Finally, brothers, whatever is true, whatever is noble, whatever is right, whatever is pure, whatever is lovely, whatever is admirable—if anything is excellent or praiseworthy—think about such things. ⁹Whatever you have learned or received or heard from me, or seen in me—put it into practice. And the God of peace will be with you.

—*Philippians 4:1–9*

Quiet time questions (Philippians 4:1–9)

1. Philippians 4:1 begins with the word *therefore*. What is it there for? Look back at Philippians 3:20–21 and write your answers.

2. a. Paul gives us some clues about the nature and work of Euodia and Syntyche. Using your imagination and these clues, write down phrases that describe these women.

   b. What might similar women be doing in your church?

3. a. If Euodia and Syntyche were to reflect on what you found in answer to question 1, how might this have helped them stop bickering?

   b. How can this help you?

Verses worth memorizing: Philippians 4:6–7

Do not be anxious about anything, but in everything, by prayer and petition, with thanksgiving, present your requests to God!

And the peace of God, which transcends all understanding, will guard your hearts and your minds in Christ Jesus.

STUDY SEVEN

Philippians 4:1–9

Muriel is up to three Excedrins
after the boys get off to school (and Charlie to work),
after she has done her daily errands,
after the nightly high jinks, confusion, and bickering of the
 supper table.
She often wonders if God has anything for her. Life seems
so unraveled and frenetic.
Perhaps through Paul's kind words on peace in this week's
passage God will help Muriel . . . and others who know what
she means.

Read Philippians 4:1–9 aloud.

1. From a reading of these verses, what problems do you
 suspect troubled the Philippians? _____

 _____

 _____

2. a. Mention all the instances in these verses in which Paul's warm affection for the Philippians is evident.

_____

_____

_____

  b. How might this loving support have influenced their outlook and their actions? _____

_____

_____

_____

3. In what ways does Paul try to heal the rift between Euodia and Syntyche (vv. 1–3)? _____

_____

_____

_____

Focus on verses 4–7.

4. a. Why do you think Paul repeated his command to rejoice? _____

_____

_____

  b. From the passage, what do you suspect are some barriers to rejoicing? _____

_____

_____

  c. Going through verses 4–7 in order, note all the reasons we have to rejoice. _____

_____

_____

_____

5. a. What have you noticed to be particular causes of anxiety? _____

_____

   b. How are you affected by anxiety? _____

_____

_____

6. What are Paul's alternatives to anxiety, and why would they be effective? _____

_____

_____

_____

7. Have you ever been startled by God's peace in the midst of severe problems? _____

_____

_____

_____

Read verses 8–9 aloud again.
8. What have you noticed happens when a person does not follow the instructions of verse 8? _____

_____

_____

_____

9. In what ways do daily, private Bible study and prayer help fulfill the command of verses 8–9? _____

_____

_____

10. a. How do the three main paragraphs we have been studying (vv. 2–3, 4–7, and 8–9) each emphasize peace? _____

_____

_____

_____

_____

   b. Think of a place where you are currently not very peaceful. Mention a clue this passage gives you about tackling the problem. _____

_____

_____

_____

Follow-up project:
   Think of someone who needs your support. Write him or her a note that will be encouraging.

Alternate project:
   1. List ten of your current anxieties. Check the dominant one and also the one that you have suppressed and don't think about.
   2. Use the model suggested by Paul in verses 4–6 to bring these before the Lord.

3. Finally, list ten things about the circumstances of your life that meet the requirements of verse 8. Thank the Lord for these things. Then post your list in a prominent place where you will be reminded of them frequently during the day.

Thanks for Their Gifts

[10]I rejoice greatly in the Lord that at last you have renewed your concern for me. Indeed, you have been concerned, but you had no opportunity to show it. [11]I am not saying this because I am in need, for I have learned to be content whatever the circumstances. [12]I know what it is to have plenty. I have learned the secret of being content in any and every situation, whether well fed or hungry, whether living in plenty or in want. [13]I can do everything through him who gives me strength.

[14]Yet it was good of you to share in my troubles. [15]Moreover, as you Philippians know, in the early days of your acquaintance with the gospel, when I set out from Macedonia, not one church shared with me in the matter of giving and receiving, except you only; [16]for even when I was in Thessalonica, you sent me aid again and again when I was in need. [17]Not that I am looking for a gift, but I am looking for what may be credited to your account. [18]I have received full payment and even more; I am amply supplied, now that I have received from Epaphroditus the gifts you sent. They are a fragrant offering, an acceptable sacrifice, pleasing to God. [19]And my God will meet all your needs according to his glorious riches in Christ Jesus.

[20]To our God and Father be glory for ever and ever. Amen.

Final Greetings

[21]Greet all the saints in Christ Jesus. The brothers who are with me send greetings. [22]All the saints send you greetings, especially those who belong to Caesar's household.

[23]The grace of the Lord Jesus Christ be with your spirit.

—*Philippians 4:10–23*

Quiet time questions (Philippians 4:10–23)

1. Read Philippians 4:10–23. List reasons Paul and the Philippians have for contentment.

2. Scan the Book of Philippians and see whether you can find a half-dozen reasons why the average person might be discontent.

3. What do you think is the relation between a person's contentment and his desire to give to others?

STUDY EIGHT

Philippians 4:10–23

Do you feel good about yourself and your circumstances? Chances are that, like most of us, you have mixed feelings. You are contented with some things and not with others.

Fact is, most of us have not found deep satisfaction despite such things as family, income, or possessions. Millionaire Andrew Carnegie was asked how much it took to make a person happy. "Just a little bit more," he replied.

The apostle Paul would have had less to declare on his income tax than most of us. Yet he claimed to experience a level of contentment we seldom know. Somehow or other he had found a key to contentment that has eluded us. Let's see if we can discover what it is.

Read Philippians 4:10–23 aloud.

1. What elements in the Philippians' behavior cause Paul to rejoice (vv. 10–20)? _____

_____

_____

_____

_____

2. What have we studied so far that helps us to understand Paul's circumstances and the "troubles" the Philippians shared with him? (See 1:7, 13, 20; 2:17, 21.) _____

_____

_____

_____

3. What was the nature of the Philippians' sharing with him? (See 2:25–30; 4:14–18.) _____

_____

_____

_____

_____

Now focus on verses 10–13.
4. a. Under what different circumstances does Paul seem to feel he needs strength? _____

_____

b. Does it surprise you that Paul needs divine strength in time of plenty? Explain your answer. _____

_____

_____

_____

5. What problems have you experienced with handling abundance in a godly way? _____

_____

_____

_____

_____

6. Suppose a person experiencing hard times said, "I asked God to change things and nothing happened." Using these verses, how would you answer his complaint?

_____

_____

_____

_____

7. How was Paul's contentment different from a merely fatalistic acceptance of hard times? _____

_____

_____

Focus on verses 14–20.
8. The Philippians had given Paul a gift.
   a. Because of this, what conclusion does Paul draw about them? _____

   _____

   _____

   b. Of what significance to God is this gift? _____

   _____

   _____

9. Paul says he had learned to be content in all circumstances. Do you see any way in which his contentment increased with the arrival of Epaphroditus? _____

_____

_____

_____

10. From what Paul says about the ways God meets needs, what might the Philippians expect about his meeting of their needs? (Use the whole passage.) _____

_____

_____

_____

11. Do you see your situation in life as one of want or of plenty? _____

How, in the light of this passage, might God help you?

_____

_____

12. Think of one person, here or abroad, with material or personal needs. _____

How might you enter into partnership with that person as the Philippians and Paul did with each other? _____

_____

_____

Follow-up project:

Name a person whom you or your church thinks of as a special representative in another country. List concrete ways you can express your partnership with this person. Choose one way and do it.

Quiet time questions (Philippians summary study 1)

1. Now that we have finished studying Philippians bit by bit, read through the entire letter rapidly to get a sense of its wholeness. After all, Paul intended that the Philippians read it at one sitting.
2. Write a list of the ideas you see repeated.

3. What concepts in the Book of Philippians are you thankful for?

Spend time thanking God for these things.

STUDY NINE

Philippians survey 1

Charlie Brown thinks puppies are the greatest. And what red-blooded American would disagree? Curling up in a corner with our childhood version of Snoopy may be one of our best memories.

Yet most of us would not hold it against God if he prepared even greater delights for our adult life. So far we may have experienced them only as a will-o'-the-wisp or pleasures glimpsed only at a distance. More likely some solid joys have been our daily friends.

One of the most engaging teachings of the Bible is that God still has joys for us that we do not know. In fact, he guarantees that some of his finest gifts have yet to come. Whatever else can he mean when he encourages us to "grow" in Christ? Surely growing nearer to him will enlarge our joy.

Good theory. But how can it impregnate our daily lives with the abundance so evident in God's promises? One way we can make progress here is to study the most joyful of all

Paul's letters to see why joy was such a factor in his life. Maybe his experience of joy will rub off on us.

1. a. Scan Philippians, underlining all references to joy, rejoicing, and being glad.

   b. Divide these references into two groups by making a √ by all those that refer to Paul and an X by all the ones that refer to the Philippians.

2. a. For each reference to Paul's joy (gladness, cheer) write the reason why Paul is rejoicing. Share the reasons you found with the group. _____

   _____

   _____

   _____

   b. How would you summarize Paul's reasons for being glad? _____

   _____

   _____

3. What does Paul's rejoicing tell you about his sense of values? _____

   _____

   _____

   _____

4. How do things that cause you to rejoice differ from Paul's?

   _____

   _____

   _____

5. What is the effect on our rejoicing if we do not value the noble things Paul valued? _____

_____

_____

_____

6. a. Mention a number of circumstances from this letter that could have caused Paul to be disheartened but did not.

_____

_____

b. Why do you find that he was not disheartened by them? _____

_____

_____

_____

7. a. How do we know from this letter that Paul did experience sorrow and anxiety? _____

_____

_____

_____

b. How do you square this with statements elsewhere in the letter about his contentment? _____

_____

_____

_____

8. a. What reasons do you personally have for sorrowing or being anxious? _____

_____

_____

_____

b. How does Philippians help you to maintain your equilibrium or even be joyful in the midst of these sorrows and anxieties? _____

_____

_____

_____

Follow-up project:
Paul rejoiced in his warm association with the Philippians and also in God's work in the Philippians, in himself, and in the world generally (the gospel was being preached, for example).

1. Find parallels in your own life that lead you to rejoice.

2. Express your delight to God in these matters.
3. Paul shared his joy with the Philippians. Share your joys with someone this week.

Quiet time questions (Philippians summary study 2)

Read Philippians as though you had never heard of Jesus Christ before.

1. What major things do you learn about him?

2. How would you like to be different because of what you learned about him?

3. What would you like to thank and praise him for?

4. Pray, using your answers to questions 2 and 3.

STUDY TEN

Philippians survey 2

Years ago *His* magazine published a story about a girl named Mary. When Mary was five, her mother died. The preacher said, "The Lord giveth and taketh away." Mary wondered if that wasn't Indian giving.

At ten Mary found that daddy became angry if she told him her problems. Since God said, "Honor your father," Mary started telling him only about happy things.

At fifteen Mary was promised a car by daddy if she got straight A's. It didn't give her much time to make friends, but she thought it was worth it. At church the preacher said righteousness is a gift and then discussed the budget.

At eighteen Mary decided to go to school near home so she could keep house for daddy. They read the Bible together each morning.

At twenty Mary found that the young adult class didn't understand her comments. This made her feel lonely, even in church.

At twenty-two Mary started crying at work one day and couldn't stop. They called it a nervous breakdown. "Don't worry, Mary's always been a good girl," the preacher said. The Sunshine Committee at church sent Mary a potted plant and a get-well card.

Relationships count. If they're deep, they build us up. If they're shallow, they destroy us, just as they destroyed Mary. Let's learn to be in touch, not just in contact. This week we'll pull together the ideas on relationships God shows us through Paul. Let's look at evangelism, prayer, harmony, and interest in others.

1. Paul calls the Philippians his partners in 1:5. What other words do you find in this letter that express partnership?

   _____

   _____

Evangelism

2. One way the Philippians were partners with Paul was in evangelism. Think through the passages that deal with their mutual involvement in this task. How do you think evangelism can forge a strong bond between Christians?

   _____

   _____

   _____

   _____

Prayer

3. In light of the reasons we see people praying in Philippians (1:4; 1:9–10; 1:19; 4:6), what case can you make

for prayer as an essential part of a relationship? _____

_____

_____

_____

_____

Harmony

4. Considering all the things Paul says Christians have in common, why, according to him, do we have trouble getting along happily? _____

_____

_____

5. For what reasons does Paul see harmony among Christians as a goal of special value? (Consider 1:9–11; 1:27–30; 2:5–11; 2:12–13; 4:1–2.) _____

_____

_____

_____

6. Think of a relationship with a Christian in which you have trouble getting along. _____

What practical thing might you do to improve this relationship? _____

_____

_____

_____

Interest in others

7. Looking out for the interests of others is a crucial part of a

relationship. Identify the passages in this book where people act out of concern for others. _____

_____

_____

8. For the people involved in each of these cases, what was the cost of serving others? _____

_____

9. When we open our homes in the service of others, what can we expect will be some of the costs? _____

_____

_____

10. In what ways does the Book of Philippians suggest that the satisfactions outweigh the costs? _____

_____

_____

_____

11. Suppose someone in your fellowship group loses his or her job. How might what we have discovered about relationships in Philippians guide you in helping out? (Consider especially what you have discussed today.) _____

_____

_____

_____

Follow-up project:

This week use question 6 of the group study. Take steps to improve your relationship with the person you thought of in response to this question.

NOTES TO LEADERS

STUDY ONE

Leader's notes on Acts 16:6–24; Philippians 1:1–11

Do you feel a bit nervous about leading? You will find encouragement and substantial help in two brief sections at the beginning of the guide. They are "Getting the Most From Group Study" and "The Pleasure of Leading a Study."

Q1. Because of a vision sending him to Macedonia (v. 9). Because it was a leading city (v. 12). He was blocked from going elsewhere (vv. 6–7). He went in order to preach the gospel (v. 10).

Q2. Words and phrases that answer this question include "several days" (v. 12), "stay at my house" (v. 15), "once when we were going to the place of prayer" (sounds like more than the first time) (v. 16), "many days" (v. 18).

Q3. Read and answer the (a) and (b) parts to this question separately. (a) Encourage the group to find a number of contrasts between the two kinds of receptions Paul received. (b) Some of the reasons for these differences are: The women were worshipers of

God, meeting for prayer, and the Lord opened their hearts (v. 14). The owners of the slave girl, on the other hand, lost their profit and charged the disciples with disturbing the city and advocating practices not in accord with Roman law.

Q4. Though not preventing the imprisonment of Paul and Silas, God set them free by an earthquake and even used it to convert the jailer and his household. God also brought about a public apology from the magistrates for their imprisonment and beating.

Q5. Ask part (a) and discuss the answers to it before going on to part (b). These answers are especially important because they set the stage for this week's study in Philippians 1:1–11. Possible answers: (a) They knew that hard times would come, but God was able to preserve them in the midst of them. (b) They would have a feeling of warm gratitude toward Paul for risking his life for their salvation.

Q6. God has continued to preserve them. They've grown in number and have had to become more organized. This is indicated by the letter's being addressed to "all" the saints and to a church with "overseers and deacons."

Q7. He remembers them often and prays for them with thanksgiving and joy. He feels they are his partners and depends on their support. He holds them in his heart and longs for them affectionately.

Q8. Paul's enthusiasm is justified, because their concern for each other is genuine and not superficial. The Philippians have shown persistent partnership with him from the first day to the present (v. 5); it was *God* who began a good work in them (v. 6); and it is this same God who will carry it through to completion. They all share in God's continuing grace in living out the gospel.

Q9. (1) The part knowledge and insight play in their love must increase. (2) They must discern what God calls "best." (3) Their own personal righteousness must grow out of this discernment. To God, "completion" refers to morality and indicates the need for repentance and holiness (fruits of righteousness) that glorify him.

Q10. Paul's love for the non-Christians at Philippi showed insight in that on his arrival he looked for the place where people showed genuine interest in prayer (at the river). He showed himself to be filled with righteousness in that after being unjustly jailed, he continued to praise God by singing. He showed insight into God's ways after the earthquake by refusing to run, but rather staying to encourage the jailer and then to explain the gospel to him. He showed insightful love for the Philippian church by insisting on a public apology. As a result, the antagonistic rulers changed their attitude and tried to appease them. This put the government more on the side of the little church Paul left behind. In Philippians 1, Paul discerns what is best in the Philippians and so thanks God for these traits. Also, his warmhearted support of them shows his abounding love.

Q11. Sometimes it is difficult to be specific about the way God is developing moral character in us: somehow it seems like a form of bragging. But God helps us to believe we are his by producing righteousness in us that is not our own. Help the members of your group to be specific. Perhaps one member will be able to think of ways she sees God at work in another member.

STUDY TWO

Leader's notes on Philippians 1:12–26

> Do you feel a bit nervous about leading? You will find encouragement and substantial help in two brief sections at the beginning of the guide. They are "Getting the Most From Group Study" and "The Pleasure of Leading a Study."

Q1. This question is to help your group members more vividly imagine the Philippians' state of mind as they received this letter from Paul when he was far away, in prison, cut off from them.

Q2. He's despondent because he's in prison: he's confined to one spot, can't make his own schedule, is controlled by his enemies. He might fear his imprisonment will frighten other Christians into silence (vv. 12–14). Some believers seem to dislike him so much they take pleasure in flaunting their freedom to preach when he is so severely restricted; they seem to have enjoyed hurting Paul

(v. 17). He could be discouraged because the outcome of his trial is uncertain; he could be executed (v. 20). He might fear he won't be able to visit the Philippians again (vv. 24–25).

Q3. The gospel has been advanced. The whole of Caesar's guard and all the rest in the palace have come to know that Paul is in prison because of his belief in Jesus Christ. In addition, most of the Roman Christians have become more confident and witness with boldness. Christ is being proclaimed (v. 18), and no matter what the outcome, Christ will be honored (v. 20).

Q4. Just as fire in the midst of deadwood is not itself threatened but has an effect on the wood, the believers found that the gospel in the palace through the presence of Paul was firing the imagination of the guard and the other officials there. Through the gospel they saw the power of God to produce change. Not only the effect on the guard, but the example of Paul would have encouraged the believers in Rome; he did not give up, so neither would they.

Q5. God presents his gospel in the face of seemingly overwhelming odds. It is successful even when chained down, among its enemies, and despite the corrupt motives of some of its preachers.

Q6. There is power in the gospel. If we turn it loose by talking about Christ, it makes its own way. This would be true even among those we wouldn't expect to listen, or when the penalty for speaking could be severe. Even when we are afraid, are not sinless, or suspect our motives may be mixed, God can use the news about Jesus powerfully.

Q7. He anticipates rejoicing in the Philippians' prayerful concern for him and in the continued help of the Holy Spirit (v. 19). He expects to be able to face whatever comes, unashamed and with courage (v. 20). He rejoices that Christ will continue to be honored. He sees value in either choice that faces him—dying, which will bring him into the Lord's presence, or living, which will reunite him with the Philippians.

Q8. (a) He is concerned that Christ will be exalted in him (v. 20). He wants to be with Christ (v. 21), but he also wants to encourage their progress and joy in the faith (v. 25).

(b) Paul's relation to Christ was more important than the circumstances. It was Christ who was central in his life. He never saw circumstances apart from the presence, power, and guidance of the Lord. Christ was stronger than those who ignored, derided, or imprisoned him.

Qs. 9 and 10. These questions are closely linked together: (9) identifies our fears about death and (10) helps us to handle them. As members of the group identify their fears and sorrows, they may not be able to wait to find answers until you reach question 10. In that case, you may wish, after any fear is noted by the group, to ask what principles in the passage can help solve this problem. This means you will ask question 10 several times as fears are raised, rather than waiting until question 9 is completely answered.

Possible answers to question 9 include: fear of the unknown, fear that we are forgotten by God, fear that God isn't in control. Here are some other answers: Sorrow at leaving the beauty and friendships of this life. Regret for things undone. Unwillingness to cause others pain. Fear that those we are responsible for will be unprotected, overburdened, deprived of any other service we have been performing for them. Concern for the resulting loneliness or helplessness of others. Apart from these things, we may be less afraid of death itself than of the process of dying with its pain, indignities, and expenses.

An illustration of an answer to question 10: Consider a married woman's fear of leaving a family without a wife and mother. In the midst of these fears she could find joy by realizing that just as Paul served the interests of God with the churches, so she has been serving the interests of God with her family. Her ministry is not a private one, but one God has carried out through her and is able to fulfill after her departure. Christ is able to work through others to bring his presence and guidance to the family she leaves. "He who began a good work . . . will carry it on to completion" (v. 6).

Q11. When our relation to Christ is central, we see all of our activities as being done in his presence and for him. If he has called us to our routine, we honor him by doing our jobs faithfully. Pleasing him in this way becomes our goal.

However, our routine also often includes others. With Christ we can learn to serve them as whole people. Furthermore, every hour of our life is not taken up with routine; we can choose some activities that will please Christ and provide opportunities for creative service. For instance, a woman's Bible study might break the routine of household chores and put us in touch with other women whom we can serve.

STUDY THREE

Leader's notes on Philippians 1:27–2:11

> Do you feel a bit nervous about leading? You will find encouragement and substantial help in two brief sections at the beginning of the guide. They are "Getting the Most From Group Study" and "The Pleasure of Leading a Study."

Q1. Terms you might expect your group to find include: stand firm, contending as one man ("striving side by side," RSV), not being frightened by opponents. The outcome concerns destruction and salvation. The Philippians are engaged in "the same struggle" as Paul and are to suffer for Christ's sake. (Don't be satisfied with one or two answers; encourage your group to keep looking until they find them all.)

Q2. He wants their lives to reflect the nobility of the gospel. To do this they need to stand firmly united, strive with singleness of purpose, be unafraid, and view their suffering, not as a burden, but as a privilege God grants them.

Q3. (a) Answers suggested by these verses are selfish ambition, conceit, lack of humility, considering yourself better than others, paying attention only to your own interests or needs or virtues.

(b) Commitment to Christ as Lord renounces a life centered in self for one governed by him and his interests. His love for others draws us to love others for his sake.

Q4. (a) Because we are united with Christ we have his resources to encourage us. We also have the comfort from his love that makes us generous to others. We have experienced the Spirit personally and have been led into a new and noble life. We have experienced some tenderness and compassion already and recognize this as a higher way than selfishness or indifference. All these are like a taste of the pudding that shows us how satisfying it can be.

Q5. Although Jesus was very high, enjoying the privileges of being God, he came to earth as a man to serve us, even to the extent of a humiliating death for our sakes.

Q6. (a) Answers in verse 6. (b) Answers in verses 7–8.

Q7. (a) He gave up an environment of sinlessness in heaven. He gave up the recognition and honor of his deity. He gave up freedom and accepted such limitations as hunger and tiredness. In heaven all the angels honored him as God and gave thanks to him.

(b) Jesus, who created the world, subjected himself to it. He had to move from place to place by walking. He had to put up with his own creatures when they jeered him. He had to grow up and, once grown, work for a living. He had to come into intimate association with sinful people. He had to experience a humiliating death.

Q8. A Philippian could picture himself on that final day, standing at Christ's side while all his enemies were forced to admit Christ's sovereignty. A Philippian Christian could see how ashamed he'd be if in this life he had ascribed more power to Christ's earthly enemies than to Christ himself. In following Christ, he would be following a winner.

Q9. Christ had none of the sins that all of us must acknowledge. The passage says he was in very nature God, and therefore possessed God's attributes (v. 6). He showed his humility by *sacrificing* his rights as God in order to create a unified body of believers who would glorify God.

Q10. There are various kinds of servanthood. Christ was certainly no doormat for others. He had great conviction and nobility. He "became *obedient* to death." It's not that he gave in to people helplessly and let them kill him; rather he was in control, even of his own death, as he chose to be obedient to God the Father.

Q11. In answering this question, members should use their personal experiences and the discussion of the passage so far.

Q12. The passage does not oppose enthusiam or persistence. It does oppose selfishly ambitious, conceited, or self-centered attitudes that can easily arise when a Christian becomes eagerly committed to a cause. The word in the original that is translated "selfish ambition" in verse 3 has particularly in mind those who are likely to have a ministry as movers and shakers—people who are eager to get things done—but then get carried away into selfishness.

STUDY FOUR

Leader's notes on Philippians 2:12–30

Do you feel a bit nervous about leading? You will find encouragement and substantial help in two brief sections at the beginning of the guide. They are "Getting the Most From Group Study" and "The Pleasure of Leading a Study."

Last week we discovered in 2:1–11 that Paul was concerned about unity at Philippi. He said disunity is caused by a lack of the kind of humility Christ showed. In this week's passage, Paul calls on the Philippians to obey in this humble way (v. 12–16). Our questions this week seek to bring this out.

Q1. The heart of the answer is found in verses 2 and 5. It concerns Paul's call for unity. This comes only through humility of the sort Christ displayed. So the command is for unity through humility.

Q2. It is more significant that they obey God when Paul is absent than when he is present (v. 12). But they can take heart because, although Paul is absent, it is God himself who is present. He will inspire and help them to achieve his purposes.

The group may run into a problem in dealing with verse 12. Is Paul telling the Philippians they need to save themselves? (Don't raise the problem if the group doesn't.)

The answer is that God saves us when we trust ourselves to Christ. This is the meaning of being saved by grace, not works (Ephesians 2:8–9). He gives us his favor when we *don't* deserve it. But once we have salvation, we want to fulfill its implications. God has forgiven us and put his Spirit in us. Now we respond with thankfulness at being saved, and we follow his commands—that is, we "work out our own salvation." So salvation is in a believer's past, but it reaches into his present and future, too.

Q3. We find the character of God to be awesome, so he imparts this same awesomeness to anything he does or wishes us to do. For instance, though the Philippians face opponents whose power frightens them (1:28), they are intimately involved with a far greater power that will finally force even God's enemies to acknowledge the superiority of Christ (2:9–11).

Q4. For instance, you might be overwhelmed by God's power. As you try to obey God in your job, you might then feel less threatened by the power of others who tried to force you to sin.

Q5. His primary examples are Timothy and Epaphroditus, but secondarily he mentions himself and the Philippians in verses 17–18.

Q6. "Crooked and depraved" are to describe the world, while "blameless and pure" are to describe the children of God. Suppose the members of a church are characterized by complaining. Then a non-Christian might say, "They're no different than we are, so why should we commit ourselves to their Christ?" This church's doctrinal purity and stand against sin don't show up in the personal relations between its members.

Q7. He feels that it has been worth it. He is confident that the Philippians will remain true to the faith and that his life and death will not have been for nothing. Their faith is such a grand thing to him that he feels honored to join them in it by the grace of God. He trusts also that his death will serve to advance the gospel and increase their faith.

Q8. A personal response question.

Q9. There is no need to conduct a verse-by-verse search through the chapter to find the ideal traits of character Timothy illustrates. This would take too long. But as the group sees Timothy's characteristics, they should relate these to some of Paul's ideas. For instance, Timothy is genuinely anxious for the welfare of others and for the interests of Christ, reflecting Paul's command in verses 3 and

4. One can see him completing Paul's joy as it is urged in verse 2 by devotedly serving with him. He displayed the mind of Christ.

Q10. Consider attitudes toward Paul and toward the church as well as those toward God and about himself. A class member might say, for instance, "Epaphroditus would need real affection for Paul to have worked in such close association with him. That's why Paul spoke so warmly of him in verse 25."

Q11. He didn't just feel; he acted. For instance, he risked his life to get to Paul; now he is ready to take the difficult trip back to the Philippians to set their fears at rest.

Q12. Clues for the personal application of this question have been in the air through all of chapter 2. Here are a few: Keeping in touch with the love and humility of Christ through reading about him in Scripture; learning from the example of other Christians; asking God for an awareness of the battle we are in together that makes it important for us to support one another. Paul has said God is effectively working in us, both to will and to achieve. In this Bible study, if God has warmed your heart toward his picture of unity, then you are experiencing his energetic action in you (v. 13). Now, as you try to obey by thinking of practical ways to serve others, you can count on his power.

Project planning: Before the group leaves the study, read over the Follow-up Project for the coming week. Divide into working groups of two or three people. Be sure everyone is included in a group. All you need to do now is to form the groups; they can do their work later.

STUDY FIVE

Leader's notes on Philippians 3:1–11

Do you feel a bit nervous about leading? You will find encouragement and substantial help in two brief sections at the beginning of the guide. They are "Getting the Most From Group Study" and "The Pleasure of Leading a Study."

Q1. Rather than being wise counselors to the Philippians, they are predatory, self-seeking, and destructive.

Q2. Those in verse 3 are not trusting a ritual; rather, they are characterized by a certain attitude toward God. They are borne to God in worship by the Spirit. They glory in the person of Christ, not basing their worship on physical circumcision or glorying in it.

Q3. He would say that to trust a physical act is a mistake. The signs of acceptance with God are more inward and deal with our attitudes toward God and appreciation of Christ. Paul expands on this idea in Romans 2:28–29. When the group has answered this question from Philippians, read the Romans passage aloud for summary and emphasis.

Q4. Through the phrase "a Hebrew of Hebrews" Paul refers to his pedigree; beyond this he refers to his performance.

Q5. (a) If the group is confused about the meaning of Paul's phrases, these explanations may prove helpful: "On the eighth day" means Paul's father and mother had him circumcised by a rabbi, officially launching him in the way of life prescribed by the Mosaic law; "of the people of Israel" gives his genealogical and religious heritage; "the tribe of Benjamin" was an elite group within Israel because Benjamin was a favored son of Jacob; "Hebrew of Hebrews" tells us that both his parents were full-blooded Jews and not just converts; as "a Pharisee" Paul belonged to a religious party that prided itself on adhering to the letter of the law.

In answering the question, a member of the group might note that to be of the "people of Israel" could mean that a person came from a long line of Christians. To be "of the line of Benjamin" might mean that he was especially proud of his particular denomination.

(b) Concerning religious performance, Paul's zeal (v. 6) might be matched today by a fine record of church involvement. "Legalistic righteousness" might be seen today in someone who says, "I'm a good person. God would never condemn *me!*"

Q6. (a) He came to treat them as loss and as rubbish. (b) It deprives us of two things: knowing Christ Jesus and having true righteousness.

Q7. One kind of righteousness comes from what Paul did: he lived a moral life and paid attention to religious observances. It was a *self*-righteousness. He once thought he could *earn* standing with God by accumulating merit. The other kind of righteousness is given to us by God apart from our performance (v. 9). He gives it to us when we put our faith in Christ. It is not *self*-righteousness, but *Christ*-righteousness. One requires some kind of personal activity; the other is a gift from God that comes to those who recognize the ineffectiveness of their own goodness and therefore trust Christ.

Q8. Confidence in my ability to think or to keep life organized and running smoothly; confidence in my moral reputation—"I'm a good person"; confidence in others' high evaluation of me.

Q9. A member of the study may now realize that she has been trusting her life to the wrong things, as Paul once had. So she may be wondering how to shift over to the new basis. This question allows members of the group who have made the shift to talk about the act of putting their trust in Christ for salvation. See Romans 10:9.

Q10. Basically all Paul's purposes are now wrapped up in Christ. Paul is captivated by him; he sees that all the fine things in life come to him through believing in Christ. Encourage group members to express how knowing Christ makes their lives richer.

Commentary note: "And so, somehow, to attain to the resurrection from the dead" may cause some problem with your group. If it does, point out that it simply means that Paul is ready to lay hold of any method to attain the resurrection, even counting everything of previous value to him as rubbish.

STUDY SIX

Leader's notes on Philippians 3:12–4:1

Do you feel a bit nervous about leading? You will find encouragement and substantial help in two brief sections at the beginning of the guide. They are "Getting the Most From Group Study" and "The Pleasure of Leading a Study."

Q1. Some of the feeling words that may be mentioned are urgency, persistence, enthusiasm, drive, devotion ("I won't let anything stand in my way"). Elicit several answers from your group. The terms in the passage that contribute to this feeling of expectancy include "press on," "straining forward," "goal," and "prize."

Q2. This paragraph is built around a contrast that Paul repeats twice—not this action, but rather that action. In answering this question, your group should see this contrast and the emphasis Paul gives it by repetition.

Q3. He has to resist the temptation to think he is already perfect (v. 12), the temptation to dwell on past mistakes and therefore to give up (v. 13), and the temptation to let slip the progress he has already made (v. 16). "I've already arrived; I can't succeed, because I can't escape my past; I'll trade these demanding goals for more enticing ones."

Q4. A person can be so emotionally tied by sorrow and regret for the past that she is not able to take initiative in the present. Also, failure can make us so aware of our inadequacy that we don't risk trying again. We may even doubt that *God* can deliver us because we didn't find deliverance before. Group members probably will have some personal examples to share.

Q5. Because Christ Jesus has made Paul his own, capturing him for a whole new way of life (v. 12), Paul can rest in his acceptance and not be preoccupied with past sin. (You or someone in the group may also point out that according to verse 9 in last week's study, Paul is not trusting in his past performance. Rather, he trusts the righteousness from God that depends on faith in Jesus Christ.) Looking to the future, Paul sees that God's prize is worth striving for (v. 14). If our motives are sincere, we can count on God to show us when we get off track (v. 15b).

Q6. A personal response question.

Q7. Some people were living a life that contrasted sharply with one that honors Christ.

Q8. "We like to eat." "Sex is enjoyable." "Drunkness is relaxing." "The here and now is all there is, so let's live life with gusto."

"God gave us these desires and meant us to use them." "After all, who are we hurting?"

Q9. The enemies of Christ place too much value on the stomach and earthly things that pass away. The consequence of this lifestyle is destruction. The followers of Christ are committed to long-term values. These are anchored in heaven and relate to the enduring qualities true of Christ's "glorious body" and his ultimate control. So the values of the two styles of life are short term *versus* long term, and the consequences are destruction *versus* salvation.

Q10. Paul seemed to feel that to combat the evil influence of aggressive non-Christians, living a godly life was as essential as his written instruction. This question aims at helping group members identify both biblical teaching and current influential examples that have shaped their lives. Get examples of each from several people in the group. Living examples give vivid flesh-and-blood meaning to written instructions. We can see how the teaching looks when it is living and talking. On the other hand, written instructions highlight the basic point an example makes. We need both.

Q11. In commenting on this statement, encourage members of the group to identify the people for whom they are most likely to be models.

Q12. A personal response question.

STUDY SEVEN

Leader's notes on Philippians 4:1–9

Do you feel a bit nervous about leading? You will find encouragement and substantial help in two brief sections at the beginning of the guide. They are "Getting the Most From Group Study" and "The Pleasure of Leading a Study."

Q1. This question is to help the group begin to get a feel for the passage. Get answers from as many people as possible. Ask each person to say where she sees her idea expressed in the passage. Some possible answers: A disagreement between two notable women in the church and a tendency of the church to be exasperated with them and to cut them off (v. 3); tendency to be downhearted, harsh, or anxious (vv. 5–6). They may lack peace (v. 7) and be preoccupied with the failure of others (v. 8) and forget about the teaching and example of Paul (v. 9).

Q2. This is most obvious in 4:1, but the group may also see affectionate, pastoral overtones in Paul's subsequent statements. We all respond to each other's concern and high regard by making our best efforts to live up to this opinion and not to disappoint one another.

Q3. He appeals to them directly and reminds the Philippians of how these two have had a vital part in the life of the church. Your group needs to see that there are two prongs to the "making of peace"—the broader community and the individuals directly concerned both play a part.

Q4. This question asks for a personal opinion, but answers should be supported from the passage. (a, b) Paul's call to be gentle (or to forbear, v. 5), suggests there were irritating or cantankerous people at Philippi. Some might have said they were too anxious to rejoice; some might have felt they had nothing to be thankful for.

(c) "In the Lord" suggests either the source of or the atmosphere for rejoicing. Because the Lord is near (or "at hand"), we can rejoice at his accessibility. We can rejoice that he wants to receive our requests. By reflecting on his work in the past, we can see good reasons for being thankful. We can rejoice that he promises peace.

Q5. This question helps to involve group members in a more personal way with the subject of this study.

Q6. Paul's alternatives are found directly in the passage. A discussion of their effectiveness calls for each person's own experience.

We often fail to turn to God when we are in trouble. A passage like this calls us to identify and clarify our requests, make them known to God, and do it in a spirit of thankfulness based on what he has already done. It reminds us of his nearness and his interest in us.

Q7. Those who have found God's peace to be more than they expected may wish to tell the group something of the circumstances. Brevity is desirable here if you are to have time to cover the rest of this study adequately.

Q8. Each in your group will have her own ideas, such as: she may become overly critical of people around her; she may become possessed of sinful thoughts; she loses her peace.

Q9. When we read the Bible, our minds are continually alerted to the character and actions of God and to reasons for thankfulness and hope. This helps us with verse 8. Further, by reading the Bible daily we face the instruction and example of those appointed by God to teach us. So Bible reading gives us concrete ways to control our thoughts and actions.

Q10. In verses 2–3 Paul seeks to bring about peace between two women who are at odds with one another; in 4–7 he seeks to replace anxiety with peace; and in 8–9 Paul relates the God of peace to what we think about and to his own teaching and example.

Part (b) of this question helps us to relate Paul's teaching and example to current situations.

STUDY EIGHT

Leader's notes on Philippians 4:10–23

Do you feel a bit nervous about leading? You will find encouragement and substantial help in two brief sections at the beginning of the guide. They are "Getting the Most From Group Study" and "The Pleasure of Leading a Study."

Q1. An overview of the passage and a chance for everyone to participate. Keep the group together by having each one who answers mention where in the passage she sees her answer.

Revised concern (v. 10), their kindness in sharing his trouble (v. 14), their history of giving to him (vv. 15–16), the credit before God that comes to their account through their gift (vv. 17–18).

Q2. Read the verses, then summarize the nature of the problem disclosed. Paul was imprisoned by the Romans, in doubt of his life, and lacking genuine support from "friends."

Q3. The purpose of this question is to get a grasp of what the Philippians were doing for Paul. They sent him a gift, probably money (note the financial language—credit, payment), by a trusted and loved messenger who also brought Paul news about the Philippians and remained awhile to serve him.

Q4. Paul needs strength in times of plenty as well as want. We tend to think we need God's help when we are deprived of material possessions such as food, not when we have them in abundance.

Q5. Answers should be personal and specific, but brief. This is not a time to share circumstances so much as a time to share our reaction to these circumstances.

Q6. In these verses Paul is less concerned with the *material help* God gives to meet needs; he is more concerned with the *inner strength* God gives us so we can be content in the midst of needs. As the leader you may wish to ask members to illustrate this personally.

Q7. Paul sees *God* acting in his circumstances. Further, his relationship with this God is warm and personal, not cold and distant. He finds real satisfaction in knowing this God and in participating in his purposes. He is freed from complaining to contentment by God's personal action in him (v. 13).

Q8. Paul sees it as a sign of the continued affection and support for him. It is a mark of their growing spiritual maturity. And since God is no man's debtor, their gift suggests blessing will come to the Philippians (for instance, v. 17). God sees the spirit in which it is offered and is pleased.

Q9. Paul is careful to show that he could be content whether or not the gift had come, but his satisfaction with the Philippians for being kind to him seems to add a dimension to his contentment. Also, he was "filled" (RSV) and his needs were "amply supplied" (NIV) by the gift. There is the practical fact that he had money and an attentive helper now. Paul remained warm and sensitive to life, not impervious as the ideal is in some religions.

Q10. Paul's own experience is that God enables him to be content in situations of both material want and material prosperity, that he supplies the grace to face the temptations both of plenty and of short supply. He has experienced the joy of having his needs met through the material and emotional giving of caring Christians. He has been filled abundantly by these ways of God's supplying. He wants the Philippians to expect God to meet their needs in the same ways—ways that befit his power, glory, and wealth.

Qs. 11 and 12. As leader, be sure the answers are personal and specific rather than general and vague. After all, the Philippians were specific in sending Epaphroditus to meet Paul's personal need and the gift of money to meet his material need.

STUDY NINE

Leader's notes on summary study 1

Do you feel a bit nervous about leading? You will find encouragement and substantial help in two brief sections at the beginning of the guide. They are "Getting the Most From Group Study" and "The Pleasure of Leading a Study."

Q1. *Scan* does not mean to read word for word; it means "glance through." Keep the time on this question to ten minutes. When everyone has finished, quickly check references together so you all will have the same data on hand for question 2.

Q2. (a) Most of the answers are pretty straightforward. An answer to 2:17 might be more difficult: it might be something like "Joy at being one in a cause that is not in vain, but a display of the permanence of God's work in them."

(b) All these reasons for rejoicing might be summarized by saying that Paul's rejoicing is caused by his partnership with the Philippians (1:4; 2:12); by God's work in helping the Philippians grow (2:2; 2:19; 4:1, 10); by God's work with Paul (1:18b–19); and by God's work in spreading the gospel (1:18a).

Q3. He sees the progress of God's work as being the most important thing and therefore rejoices when it occurs. He sees this progress in the spread of the gospel, in the growth of young Christians, in the participation of believers in the grace and love of God, and in the control of God in his own life.

Q4. A personal response question.

Q5. We tend to attach our dreams to earthbound goals instead of heavenly goals. Paul and God were excited over the same things. Our rejoicing may be less profound, touching fewer important areas of life. For instance, if we are indifferent to relationships, we don't rejoice when God helps someone become more wholesomely related to others. If we do not value enduring things, our joy is short-lived, so we are cranky and grumbling.

Q6. The severest circumstance is probably the possibility of his death by execution. He is not disheartened because he sees that God's control will produce good results whether he lives or whether he dies. God cannot be bested.

Q7. (a) See Philippians 2:25–30, for instance. (b) As we saw in our study of 4:10–13, Paul was not indifferent to his needs, but he found strength from God to live with less than ideal circumstances.

Q8. First, we must be sure we are committed to the highest values so that we are not upset over incidentals. Second, we need to gain a high view of the importance of God and of his work in the world. Third, we need to see that God is never baffled or obstructed by circumstances; he has the power to change anything if he chooses. Fourth, we should find encouragement that when God has really begun working in a person's life, he will continue. Last, when things go sour we can trust God for the strength to persist in an even-minded way. He undergirds our lives with a contentment we can accept by faith.

STUDY TEN

Leader's notes on summary study 2

Do you feel a bit nervous about leading? You will find encouragement and substantial help in two brief sections at the beginning of the guide. They are "Getting the Most From Group Study" and "The Pleasure of Leading a Study."

Q1. Scan the book *rapidly*—about five minutes—looking for words and phrases that show partnership. Some answers are: brother, fellow worker, fellow soldier, you whom I love and long for, messenger and minister, yokefellow, fellow workers, side by side.

Q2. When we get enthusiastic about the things that concern God, we are drawn together around him. When evangelism puts one person on the spot, other people tend to set aside their prejudices and support him—as the Philippians supported Paul with a gift when he was on the spot. When a Christian holds out the word of life (2:16), others rejoice with him. The Christians involved end up with many things in common to talk about. When a non-Christian is saved, joy sweeps through the fellowship, uniting everyone.

Q3. Prayer in Philippians is for these causes: Thanksgiving for partnership (1:4), prayer for growth (1:9–11), prayer for help when someone was in trouble (1:19), prayer in time of anxiety (4:6–7). A joyful friendship is a gift from God, so he is central in it; it is based on more than our own natural liking, and we are thankful to him for its quality. The deepest part of our "self" is our relationship with God. In a genuine friendship, we wish to touch each other at this fundamental level. So when we are opposed by others or pressed by anxieties or seeking to grow in Christ, we and our friends turn to God for help.

Q4. For instance, Paul mentions envy and rivalry (1:15), selfish ambition (1:17; 2:3), vain conceit and lack of humility (2:3), indifference to the interests of others (2:4), complaining and arguing (2:14), and looking out for our own interests (2:21).

Q5. The fruits of righteousness seem to depend on insightful, discerning love. Harmony among Christians is a warning to enemies of the gospel. Harmony reflects the attitude of Christ. Harmony suggests we are all obeying the same leader; it shows we are standing firm in the gospel.

Q6. A personal response. Though each person should think of a specific person with whom she is having problems, the name of this person should probably not be shared with the group. But do discuss together the specific actions that can be taken to reestablish a more harmonious relationship.

Q7. A major reason why Paul wanted to get out of prison was to help the Philippians in their progress and joy in the faith (1:25). Timothy looked out for the interests of Paul and the Philippians, so he was willing to be Paul's representative (2:19). Because of their interest in Paul, the Philippians sent Epaphroditus with a gift (2:25; 4:14–17). Christ served us by dying on a cross (2:8).

Q8. Epaphroditus almost died. Christ did die. Timothy faced a hard journey. If Paul was released to go to the Philippians, he faced a long journey and the hardships of continued ministry. These answers may be elaborated on to convey more sense of the real meaning of each.

Q9. Time, wear and tear, lack of privacy, extra housework, more equipment (chairs, dishes), money for food, emotional involvement, and guilt over mistakes we make—these are some of the answers you may expect to this question.

Q10. Other Christians support us in our ministry, and as we work together we are drawn close to them. The phrase "to live is Christ" includes the idea that when we do his will, we have the pleasure of being identified with him (1:21). It is a privilege to endure various hardships on behalf of Christ (1:29). Part of Paul's joy was in the Philippians' response to him and in seeing God's work in them. Becoming like him in his death, we can attain the resurrection (1:21, 23; 3:10–11; 3:21).